COLOURS OF LIFE

JOURNEY OF TIME

DIVYA WADHWA

Made with ♥ on the Notion Press Platform
www.notionpress.com

Contents

Acknowledgements   *v*

About the Author   *vii*

  1. Quotes   1

Poems

  2. Dreams   7

  3. Doors Of Vision   8

  4. The Boundless Mind   9

  5. Aspirations   10

  6. Creativity   11

  7. Recognition   12

  8. Education   13

  9. Knowledge   14

10. Skills   15

11. Training   16

12. Challenge   17

13. Patience   19

14. Optimism   20

15. Wisdom Whispers   22

16. Mist   24

17. Beauty   26

18. Nature   27

19. Nurturing   28

20. Time To Shine   30

21. Accomplishment   31

Contents

22. Awesome — 32

23. Whispers Of The Heart — 35

24. Wisdom — 36

25. The Journey — 37

26. Feelings — 38

27. Gratitude — 39

28. A Gesture Of Values — 42

29. Forgiveness — 43

30. Prayers And Offerings — 44

31. Children — 45

32. Pencil And Pen — 46

33. Dimensional Acrostic — 47

34. Hands — 48

35. If I Were A Bee — 49

36. Smile — 50

37. Joy — 51

A Classical Tale

38. The Silent Struggle Of Misha — 55

Article

39. Overcoming Helplessness: A Story Of Survival — 61

Acknowledgements

This book has been an amazing journey filled with moments of exploring, learning, reading and presenting the Colours of Life, Journey of time.

First and foremost, I am grateful to the divine for motivating me and for his countless blessings bestowed upon me.

I am deeply indebted to my parents for being my source of strength.

I thank my family for their encouragement, love, and patience throughout the most challenging moments.

I appreciate the efforts of my husband and my friend Varsha Khairnar to help me in proofreading and editing my first book.

I am thankful to my mentors and friends, your insights and guidance have been invaluable for your constructive feedback, shared wisdom and constant motivation.

Special thanks go to the team behind the scenes—the editors, designers, and publishers—who helped shape my words into the finished work you now hold.

Finally, to everyone who believed in this book and contributed in any way, your contributions have made this dream a reality.

With heartfelt gratitude,
Divya Wadhwa

About The Author

Divya Wadhwa is a teacher by profession, writer by passion, a lifelong learner and an educator. Her academic background includes an MA, M.Ed., TTC, a soft skill trainer, POSH trainer, counsellor, career analyst.

Divya is working on equipping educators with tools and methodologies to inspire and engage students effectively. She emphasizes best practices in pedagogy, reflective teaching, and leveraging technology in the classroom.

Her approach integrates traditional teaching with innovative strategies like active learning, critical thinking, problem solving and soft skills.

She concentrates on building a positive classroom culture where curiosity, collaboration, and creativity thrive, encouraging students to become lifelong learners, fostering the importance of empathy, communication, and inclusive learning.

Divya is a co-author of three well-received anthologies: Rebellions, Quixotic Quorum, and Heart Strings.

Through her writing, training, and teaching, she continues to inspire and uplift budding educators, authors, and learners worldwide.

Quotes

"Calm down dear Mind, Calm down."

"Effective communication resolves many issues."

"Enrich your life with knowledge and education."

"Hone your Skills to empower self."

"Craft thinking to express your art of perspective."

"Instill values in yourself to develop your character."

"Lead by example to showcase your potential."

"Every individual has unique taste,
viewpoint, and method."

"The act of kindness is humility."

"Be a shining moment in someone's life to inspire change and hope."

"Smiling is spurred on by moments of joy and delight."

"Uniqueness is the key to success"

Poems

Dreams

Once, dreams were vibrant, bold, and bright,
Leading me through an infinite brightness.,
A future painted with vivid hues,
Endless Possibilities to embrace.

The relentless passage in time, brings profound change,
As reality's impact now abounds,
The dreams that once soared, free and true,
Slowly morph, their Colours askew.

Yet, in this transition, an opportunity arises,
Weave a new path, to evolve,
Discover the beauty in what now is,
And cherish each moment's subtle bliss.

For dreams may diminish, but purpose endures,
Reality's canvas, our canvas to paint,
With gratitude for the journey ahead,
Where hope and contentment, walk hand in hand.

Doors of Vision

Within the confines of the brain,
exist a gateway to the hidden,
an entrance way of vision,
Revealing critical thinking and creativity technique.

Exposing truth, a life beyond the boundary,
Opening and releasing doors
from perishable views,
Dwelling dreams in the heart.

Observing aspirations, the anxieties and uncertainties,
Thinking, planning, imagining innovation
The significance of perception in the universe
communicates a new perspective.

Multiple varied openings of knowledge,
Pathways lead to magical place,
while others lead to never-ending conflict.
With every stride we make, we release the entrance.

The Boundless Mind

Imagine the power of the limitless mind,
revealing facts and leaving doubts behind.
Where ideas bloom like bright flowers,
turn everyday life into enchanting towers.

Imagine the courage to take the leap,
daring to cross the trodden and deep.
Believing in the power of imagination
Disappearing fears with a new fascination.

Imagine the joy of creating a new,
Designing a true vision that grew
Where the impossible became a reality,
with your art changing the world modality.

A gift holy, boundless and true,
Forgiveness shines, a beacon to the soul,
It lifts the burden we once felt,
And sets us free, healing us whole.

Imagine, my friend, in power,
Build, explore, and conquer
For in the infinite realm of the intellect
the greatest journeys are found.

Aspirations

The desire for achieving goals, specific to you,
A path for learning and experiences,
motivating or inspiring you.

Creating the latest version of you.
Removing different obstacles and differences,
Stimulating and persuading you.

It shapes your vision,
achieving positive thinking growth.
Avoiding your confusion.

Leading to failure,
Ushering purpose and direction,
Opening doors to venture.

A life of aspirations is like
full of glory, fame, or blame,
trial and errors or just like a game.

Inspiring a light of happiness and peace,
Calming things down,
Aspirations are a step towards success.

Creativity

In an atmosphere of the immense area,
Creativity sparks, a wonderful dance,
A canvas where ideas take flight,
Reveals the world with a new light.

With bold Colours and true lines,
It always paints on the portrait, a new,
Transforming the more into the sublime,
A symphony of thought, a timeless rhyme.

Wings of limited imagination,
soar high, unlock hidden springs,
tell stories that capture the soul,
Create masterpieces that fill us.

In the realm of the creative mind
we find limitless possibilities,
a gift that empowers, inspires and ignites,
celebrates the beauty written by creativity.

Recognition

In the world of ideas, where intellect decode,
A gentle touch with recognition,
A nod of understanding, a glance so fine,
A gesture of acceptance, a bond divine.

With open hearts and minds, we begin anew,
Recognize the past, and all it is true.
The lessons learned, the memories we hold,
The love and laughter, the stories untold.

Through trials and woes, we find our way,
And in the darkness a light shines each day.
The Recognition's power, it sets us free,
Move forward, wild, and carefree.

In the present moment, we find our peace,
A sense of calm, a world to cease.
Recognition's wisdom, it guides the way,
Towards a more optimistic future,
gripping a fresh start ahead.

Education

Education is dispersing awareness,
Enhancing safe, comfortable living,
Progressing, succeeding and valuing,
With growth and prosperity.

Enlightening your minds,
Imparting learning opportunities,
Advancing knowledge, improving Health,
Extending hands to equality and peace.

Education fosters sustainability,
Integrating culture, vision and skills,
Bringing in movements of social transformation,
Influencing modern innovations with success.

Knowledge

In the boundless world of the spirit,
Knowledge, a treasure to be determined,
Beacon to guide us through the night,
Illuminate the way to endless light.

Turning each page, opening a new world,
Secrets of the past, untold stories,
A tapestry of wisdom thread by thread,
Woven enriching lives.

Knowledge, a gift that transcends time,
spreading doors to the sublime,
Whispers the truth, reveals the unknown
and empowers us to stand on our own.

In his embrace we find strength to grow,
To question, to explore, to let our thoughts flow,
For the memory, a flame that burns brightly,
To ignite our infinite spark of joy.

Skills

• 15 •

In halls of learning, where minds take flight,
A fortress of courage builds, day, and night,
The skills that slumber, awakening slow,
Like butterflies, unfold, and start to grow.

The practiced rhythms, the smooth flow,
Of fingers dancing, minds aflame, they know,
The craftsman's touch, the artist's hand,
The expert's stroke, the words to stand.

For in each skill, a story is told,
Of trials, triumphs, and moments old,
Of doubts and fears, of perseverance true,
And the quiet pride that sees it through.

So, let the education of courage build,
A sturdy foundation for the heart to fulfil.

Training

In classrooms, workshops, and fields of play,
We train and learn, day by day.
The skills we gain, the wisdom we share,
Help us grow and show us we care.

Through trials and errors, we refine,
And shape our paths, like a work of art divine.
With each step forward, we take our stand,
And build our strength, hand in hand.

For in the training of our minds and hearts,
We find the power to play our parts.
And as we rise, we help others rise,
In a journey of growth, which touches the skies.

Challenge

In the quiet dawn,
a whisper of doubt lingers,
like shadows stretching,
longing for the sunlight.

Steps falter, the path twists,
yet the heart beats louder,
a drum in the silence,
echoing, "You can."

Mountains loom,
their peaks shrouded in mist,
but each step forward etches resolve into the earth,
roots digging deep, defiant.

With every stumble, we rise,
crafting strength from the very fabric of struggle,
turning obstacles into stepping stones,
and fear into fuel.

In the crucible of challenge,
we find ourselves—
not just the fight,
but the fire that ignites our spirit,
transforming the impossible into the possible.

In moments of challenge, we find our strength,
Facing obstacles head on, no matter the length.
We rise above, we push through the pain,
For in adversity, we have much to gain.

With unwavering resolve, we stand tall,
Ready to conquer, ready to give it our all.
Through trials and tribulations, we persevere,
For we know that victory is always near.

So, bring on the challenges, let them come,
We are prepared, we are not overcome.
With courage and determination, we will prevail,
For in the face of adversity, we will never fail.

Patience

In the stillness of waiting
The lie is a soothing virtue,
A quiet force that strengthens the soul,
When the steady march of time makes its own.

Patience, a guiding light in the dark,
Lights the way without leaving a trace,
Calms the restless mind,
Reminds that peace is found.

With every breath, a lesson unfolds,
In patience, an untold story
Of growing up, of wisdom, of inner peace,
When the heart's desires quietly cease.

In this fast world, there is a rare gem,
patience, a treasure of reflection,
flood of haste, fast time,
revealing the beauty of life, sublime.

Optimism

In the darkest hour, when all seems lost,
And shadows whisper of a heavy cost,
It is optimism that shines bright,
A hope in the dead night.

Like a butterfly emerging from its cocoon,
Optimism lifts us up, like a sweet tune,
It whispers of better days to come,
And guides us through the storm, steady and calm.

With optimism, there is no room for despair,
For it fills our hearts and minds with care,
It paints a picture of a brighter tomorrow,
And banishes all traces of sorrow.

It is the light that pierces through the clouds,
And dispels all doubts, fears, and shrouds,
It is the fuel that keeps us going,
Even when the winds of change are blowing.

Optimism is the fire that burns within,
Driving us forward, helping us win,
It is the gentle hand that guides our way,
And keeps us going, day by day.

So, let us hold onto optimism tight,
And let it guide us through the darkest night,
For with its help, we can overcome,
And bask in the warmth of a brand-new sun

Wisdom Whispers

Wisdom whispers,
not in thunderous roars,
in the soft rustle of autumn leaves,
in the quiet moments between breaths,
where experience lingers,
and time unfolds its stories.

It wears the face of age,
yet dances like a child,
seeking not the loud applause,
the gentle nod of understanding,
the light in a stranger's eyes.

In the stillness,
it invites us to listen, to pause,
to embrace the tangled threads
of joy and sorrow,
woven into the fabric of our shared humanity.

In whispers of dawn,
where light spills gently,
beauty stirs - a tender breath,
a child's laughter,
the bloom of a single flower,
pushing through cracked concrete.

It dances in the eyes of strangers meeting,
in hands that reach across divides,
in the silence held between heartbeats,
where understanding grows like wildflowers
in forgotten corners.

Mist

In the quiet hours of dawn,
when the world holds its breath,
a mist unfurls like a whisper,
a veil draped over sleeping fields,
softening the edges of reality,
dissolving the lines between earth and sky.

It dances through the trees,
a ghostly figure,
twisting and twirling,
embracing the branches,
kissing the leaves with a tender touch,
shrouding the familiar in mystery.

The air is thick with secrets,
each droplet a story,
each wisp a memory,
filling the spaces between silence,
where thoughts float like feathers,
light and fleeting, lost and found.

Footsteps fade into the grey,
the path ahead obscured,
yet in this shroud of uncertainty,
there is a kind of freedom—
to wander, to wonder.
Unanchored by the weight of knowing,

To let the heart lead the way,
wherever the mist may lay,
And as the sun awakens,
casting golden fingers through the haze,
the world slowly re-emerges.
in the embrace of the mist.

Beauty

Beauty is life a holy face
unfurling like wings,
a soft, steady rain,
nurturing the roots of aim.

Appealing the senses,
Pleasing with attractiveness,
Appreciating the eternity within,
gazing at it like in a mirror.

It is not acquired in a day,
Through experiences that come our way,
In the trials and tribulations we face,
We learn to navigate with grace.

Beauty is not just a face or color,
The shine and the power within,
It is not just a thought to share,
It is like a faith to rely.

Nature

In the enormous and realistic palette of nature
A masterpiece beyond our view,
Every living, breathing, wondrous part,
A testament to nature's artistic power.

The towering trees, the flowing streams,
Blooming flowers, nature's aspirations,
All woven in a tapestry,
Of life, and everlasting harmony.

The soaring birds, the buzzing bees,
The rustling leaves, the whispering breeze,
A symphony of sights and sounds,
Brings true peace in our hearts.

Through nature's perspective, we witness the elegance,
Of a world beyond our human existence,
A natural perspective, pure and wise,
Reminding us to open our eyes.

In awe, we stand, humbled and insignificant,
Before this majestic, and towering spectacle,
Nature's gift, a treasure to cherish,
A beauty that can never be...

Nurturing

In the quiet dawn of a tender morning,
the sunlight whispers softly,
Lies the gentle art of a nurturing hand,
A touch that opens the soul.

Tiny seeds in the soil, asleep,
Awaken to a nurturing call,
With patience and care, they start to grow,
In the warmth of love, they find their glow.

Children's dreams like fragile threads,
Are woven with care in their little heads,
By those who nurture, guide, and cheer,
Turning whispers of doubt into songs of clear.

Hearts that weary, burdened with strain,
Find solace in the nurturing rain,
A kind word, a listening ear,
Can turn shadows to light, make the path clear.

Nurturing is the sun warming the day,
The gentle wind that guides the way,
It is the unseen force, tender and kind,
That fosters growth in heart and mind.

In gardens of life, where hope is sown,
Nurturing hands make it all their own,
With love as the water, patience as the soil,
They cultivate joy through dedicated toil.

The nurturers, quiet and strong,
Who help us find where we belong,
In their embrace, we rise and stand,
Forever grateful for the nurturing hand.

Time to shine

Awaited day, awaited time.
to shine one day,
It will come soon one day.
Hoping to rise with all my might.

Along with determination and dedication,
Efforts to steadily achieve the goal,
with improvement and consistency,
Awakening the spirit of enthusiasm.

Encouraging inspiring self-reflecting reinventing
innovative ideas and approaches
Creating a new positive version!
Skillfully and mindfully,

Humbly and affectionately
With ability and experience,
Nurturing creativity, imagination and reality.
For your time to come.

Accomplishment

In places of education, where thoughts soar freely,
A stronghold of bravery is constructed continuously.

The abilities that lie dormant slowly come to life.
Like butterflies, they unfold and begin to shine.

The skilled beats, the seamless movement,
Their minds are ablaze as their fingers dance.

The master's touch, the words to endure
A story is narrated in every skill.

Of challenges, successes, and memories past
Of uncertainties and worries, of genuine determination.

The tranquil sense of accomplishment perseveres
Allowing the enhancement through education.

A solid base for the heart to achieve
To win, to succeed.

Awesome

Awesome is the sunset's brilliant hue,
The way it paints the sky anew,
With shades of orange, pink, and gold,
A sight so wondrous to behold.

Awesome is the ocean's vast expanse,
Its waves crashing in a rhythmic dance,
The sound of the sea like a soothing song,
A melody that makes your heart long.

Awesome is the mountain's towering height,
Its peaks kissing the clouds in flight,
The rugged terrain and rocky slopes,
A landscape where nature evokes.

Awesome is the forests' tranquil peace,
The rustle of leaves, the whispering trees,
The scent of pine and earthy moss,
A place where serenity emboss.

Awesome is the laughter of a child,
The innocence and joy so wild,
The sound that fills the air with glee,
A sound that sets your spirit free.

Awesome is the kindness of a stranger,
The compassion that knows no danger,
The act of love and selflessness,
An example of humanity's blessedness.

Awesome is the power of forgiveness,
The ability to let go and dismiss,
The burden of anger and resentment,
A grace that brings inner contentment.

Awesome is the beauty of diversity,
The different cultures and community,
The tapestry of colours and beliefs,
A reminder that unity brings relief.

Awesome is the strength of resilience,
The ability to rise above indifference,
The courage to face adversity,
A spirit that never loses its divinity.

Awesome is the love that binds us all,
The connection that never falls,
The bond that ties us in unity,
A force that transcends all scrutiny.

So, let us embrace this feeling of awesome,
Let it fill our hearts, no matter the blossom,
For in its light, we find inspiration,
A source of joy and elation.

Let us cherish the wonders that surround,
The beauty that in every corner is found,
And let us be grateful for each moment,
For life itself is awesome, don't lament.

In a world filled with chaos and uncertainty,
There exists a powerful force called gratitude,
A feeling so profound and pure,
It has the ability to heal and renew.

Whispers of the heart

In the middle of the night
When the world is silent,
Soft and clear whispers,
Convey the heart's desire.

Talk about pure and true love,
a song about the seasons,
knitting a new block,
expressing feelings in poetry.

These whispers, these soft shadows,
awaken and illuminate the soul,
and invite us to express,
the depth of the heart.

In our quiet gatherings
these whispers are our guide,
remind us to focus,
let the heart be our true guide.

In the whispers of the heart
find courage,
embrace the love that divides,
let the spirit soar.

Wisdom

Wisdom is the voice of reason,
A soothing balm in times of pensive season,
It whispers softly in our ears,
Dispelling doubts and fears.

It teaches us the value of patience,
the beauty of acceptance,
For in every challenge lies a lesson,
A chance for growth and progression.

Let us heed the call of wisdom,
Embrace its teachings with open arms,
For in its gentle embrace,
We find solace and grace.

Let us seek to be wise,
In our words and actions, let us be concise,
For in the richness of wisdom,
We find the true essence of freedom.

Let us cherish this precious gift,
Use it to uplift and uplift,
For in the wisdom we find within,
Lies the key to a life well-lived and serene

The Journey

On the road,
On the mysterious island,
as exciting as the destination!
start this new adventure,

Accepting the challenges
ahead and
full of unique memories,
valuable lessons.

Through winding paths and endless miles
My soul goes on a wild journey,
Every step is a sign of growth,
Accepting challenges, never laziness.

The road ahead, a tapestry of dreams,
Woven of hopes and bold plans,
I walk with an unknown heart open,
I wish to fulfil my modest role.

With each emerging horizon,
new perspectives dawn, guiding sight,
expanding sight, expanding mind,
I gratefully find the gifts of the journey,
Because in this search I find myself.

Feelings

In a world of wonder and delight,
There exists a sensation so bright,
A feeling beyond compare,
A feeling so pure and rare.

This feeling is awesome, it's true,
It fills your heart with happiness anew,
It lights up your soul with its glow,
And makes your spirit overflow.

It's the feeling of awe and wonder,
Of being filled with joy like thunder,
Of feeling small in the grand scheme,
Yet knowing you're part of a supreme dream.

Gratitude

Gratitude is more than just saying thank you,
It's a deep appreciation for all that we have,
It's recognizing the blessings in our lives,
And feeling content with what we've been given.

It's easy to take things for granted,
To overlook the beauty in the everyday,
But when we pause and reflect on all we have,
We realize how truly fortunate we are.

Gratitude can be found in the simplest of things,
The warmth of the sun on our skin,
The sound of laughter filling the air,
The taste of a delicious meal prepared with care.

It's in the kindness of a stranger,
The support of a friend in times of need,
The unconditional love of family,
And the beauty of nature that surrounds us.

When we practice gratitude regularly,
We unlock a key to happiness and peace,
For gratitude has the power to shift our perspective,
And bring us closer to our true selves.

It allows us to see beyond our own struggles,
And appreciate the struggles of others,
To understand that we are all connected,
And that we are stronger when we come together.

Gratitude is a practice that requires intention,
A conscious effort to focus on the positives,
Even in the face of adversity and challenges,
For there is always something to be grateful for.

It's about shifting our mindset from lack to abundance,
From complaining to appreciating,
From resentment to forgiveness,
And from sadness to joy.

Gratitude is a gift that keeps on giving,
The more we express it, the more we receive,
For when we cultivate a mindset of gratitude,
We attract more blessings into our lives.

Let us take a moment each day,
To give thanks for all that we have,
To express our gratitude to those around us,
And to cultivate a heart full of love and appreciation.

For in the end, it is not the material possessions,
Or the achievements we accumulate,
But the relationships we nurture,
And the love we give and receive,

That truly make life meaningful and fulfilling,
So, let us embrace the power of gratitude,
And give thanks for all that we have been given,
For gratitude is the key to a life well lived.

A Gesture of Values

• 42 •

A simple act, a humble act,
Reveals the depth of the true faith of the heart,
A gesture that goes beyond the norm,
Full of changing values.

A hand outstretched in need,
An ear to listen, a heart to listen,
These little acts of kindness shine,
Reflect light, divine love.

In a world consumed by selfish gain
Such gestures stand out, hold back,
remind us of what really matters,
bonds that mend and barriers that break.

A smile, a word, a gentle touch,
These little ripples mean so much,
Because in these actions we see unfolded
beauty that can change the world.

Forgiveness

• 43 •

A gift holy, boundless and true,
Forgiveness shines, a beacon to the soul,
It lifts the burdens we once felt,
And sets us free, healing us whole.

With an open heart and compassionate grace,
Letting go of the wounds that were once defined,
Embracing each other no matter what,
Allowing the healing to gently unwind.

In the face of complaints, big and small,
forgiveness is a testimony of love,
it bridges gaps, it fixes mistakes,
it connects us to the sky above.

A power that transcends time and space,
Forgiveness transforms, renews and redeems,
It offers a chance to start over, to trace,
A path that leads to our highest dreams.

Prayers and offerings

With reverent hands and humble heart,
I bring my prayers, a sacred art,
Tributes of gratitude and grace,
To the divine, the sacred realm.

Delicate flowers, their petals spread wide,
Representing beauty in this world,
I lay them down with deepest care,
A gesture of my heartfelt prayer.

The dancing flame, a guiding light,
Illuminates the path, so bright,
A signal to the skies above,
Carrying my words of faith and affection.

In this moment of silent worship,
I feel a connection, a deep emotion,
My spirit lifted, my soul refreshed,
By the power of prayers and offerings.

Children

We are small, cute, and innocent,
aspire to reach what we like,
fun loving with different ideas,
create our world of joy.

We are smart, curious, and talented,
invent, ready to share what we make.
Crave for new notions like
as chalk and cheese.

We are young, strong and represent,
Our bonds of love, care what we sake,
Each moment holds a spark, a light,
That turns the day from grey to bright.

We are simple, pure, and bright,
to dream a new for what we wake,
See the world with wonder's view,
Cherish joy, to spread our wings.

Pencil and Pen

In the land of art and creative flair,
Lies the pen and pencil, beyond compare.
Both tools of writing, with lines so fine,
Crafting stories, one line at a time.

The pen, with ink that flows like slime,
Leaves trails of beauty, a work divine.
It writes of love, of life, of dreams,
As the words unfold, like a treasure's themes.

The pencil, with lead so soft and grey,
Sketches out visions, in a gentle way.
It draws of life, of nature's hues,
As the lines unfold, like a work anew.

Together, they dance, in perfect harmony,
Creating masterpieces, a harmony.
For the pen and pencil, a perfect pair,
A match made in heaven, without a single care.

Dimensional Acrostic

D is for Dimensions, where logic bends,
I is for Imagination, our best of friends.
M is for Mysteries, in math and more,
E is for Exams; we are always sore.
N is for Naps, a classroom delight,
S is for Scribbles, a student's plight.
I is for Ideas, that never end,
O is for Overthinking, our constant friend.
N is for Notes, we seldom review.
A is for Answers, we hope are true.
L is for Learning, despite the strain.

A is for Acting, as though we know it.
C is for Confidence, we boldly display,
R is for Recalling, what we learned today.
O is for Optimism, about passing this test,
S is for Sighs when we do our best.
T is for Teachers, who guide us along,
I is for Insights, where we sometimes go wrong.
C is for Classroom, a stage for our wit.

Hands

• 48 •

In gentle touch, the world begins to speak,
With fingers weaving stories soft and bright.
They cradle dreams, and when the shadows sneak,
They lend their strength to guide us through the night.

With hands we build, we break, we heal, we sway,
In laughter's dance, they lift the heart in flight.
They shape our lives in countless, tender ways,
A silent vow, a promise held so tight.

Yet hands can hold the weight of sorrow's chains,
In every line, a tale of love and loss.
Through calloused palms, the joy and grief remain,
Each mark a journey, every scar a cross.

So, let us honor hands, both worn and fair,
For in their grasp, we find the love we share.

If I were a Bee

• 49 •

If I were a bee
I would not be an ordinary bee but a royalty,
I would be a queen honeybee.
the largest of the bees,
the heart and the soul of the bee colony
and be the mother of the hive,
I would eat jelly nectar.
I would be busy entire day moving.
filling the empty cells of the hive.

Smile

• 50 •

Have a Smile on your face,
a nature of Happiness.
a moment of joy.

Joy

Sharing a pie or feelings,
Bringing in gift of Joy,
Spreading smiles and happiness,
Collecting moments of memories.

Just a little of cheering,
Inspiring one or thousands,
What matters the most is,
Being together with Jolliness.

Caring like a sunshine,
Bringing in gift of hope,
Ushering no to nope,
Creating a melody to outshine.

Just like a creator,
covering and displaying
its talents to explore and to know more.
spending precious time.

A Classical Tale

The Silent Struggle of Misha

In a small town nestled between rolling hills, Misha stood in the front of a dimly lit classroom, the walls adorned with faded posters of inspiring quotes that once flickered with hope. Today, however, they seemed more like a haunting reminder of dreams that had fallen flat. Misha, a resolute teacher, trainer, and coach, stared out at her students—faces half-engaged, half-disinterested—lost in a world that did not recognize her worth.

Every morning, Misha woke up at dawn, her heart heavy with the day's uncertainties. She would gaze into the bathroom mirror, her image a mosaic of fatigue and resolve. Years of trying to get acceptance and credit in a field that frequently disregarded her efforts were evident in the wrinkles on her face and the shadows beneath her eyes. The passion that formerly motivated her aspirations to change the world disappeared, giving way to a desperate struggle for survival.

Despite her professional background, Misha received a low salary. She observed that her monthly salary was insufficient to cover necessities like groceries, rent, and the odd trip to the neighborhood washes. On certain evenings, she would listen to her stomach growl while her mind raced with unpaid bills.

It was hard not to feel helpless in a system that seemed to deflate every ounce of Vigor she had poured into her work.

As a teacher, Misha dedicated herself not just to academia but to nurturing young minds. She prepared lessons that catered to every student—rallying together projects to help those who struggled while leading diverse discussions that encouraged critical thinking. After school, she would transform into a coach for the struggling soccer team, encouraging them to believe in themselves just as she did. Her heart swelled with pride when she witnessed their growth, but the accolades were fleeting, overshadowed by whispers of resignation from the school board.

"Misha, you know we can't afford to give you a raise," her principal often said, not unkindly but out of necessity. "We have to prioritize."

But Misha did not just teach; she trained them to dream, to aspire for greater than what they were conditioned to believe they could be. Yet, both recognition and respect seemed elusive. The local community viewed her role as a temporary fixture, not worthy of dignified support. To them, she was simply "Miss Misha," just another cog in the educational machinery that turned slowly yet inexorably.

In the shadows of her struggle, Misha sought out solace in the friendships she formed with other educators. They gathered at the local diner, pouring themselves into late-night coffees, sharing dreams and frustrations. Each faced their own challenges: the gym coach, who had to inspire disengaged learners; the art instructor, who had to deal with budget cuts that limited supplies; and the science teacher, who was shackled to out-of-date texts. In their unrelenting struggle to establish their value in a society that frequently disregarded their profession, they provided each other with friendship.

One evening, filled with frustration, Misha stood before her small group of friends, a fire ignited in her chest. In addition to being educators, we are dream creators! Better is what we deserve!

We deserve recognition for the efforts we pour into our students. If we do not stand up for ourselves, who will?"

Her words hung in the air, sparking a flicker of recognition in the others. They talked about tactics including planning community events that showcased students' abilities, pushing local councils to provide more financing, and contacting parents to get their support. Although it was a tentative plan, it was nevertheless a plan.

They would not just be victims of the system—together, they would fight for dignity.

The following weeks were a whirlwind of activity. Misha immersed herself in lesson plans that displayed her students' talents—art displays, science fairs, and an end-of-year talent show. Each event was a chance to engage the community, bringing parents, students, and educators together to celebrate achievements rather than merely exist in quiet desperation.

As the talent show neared, Misha wore her nervousness like a badge of honor. When the night arrived, she stepped into the gymnasium, illuminated by twinkling lights and filled with laughter and songs. The students shone brighter than any recognition she had sought, each performance echoing the unheard stories of their struggles and victories. Parents beamed, clapping with pride, and for the first time, Misha felt waves of acceptance washing over her.

Months passed, and the momentum of their efforts slowly transformed the community's perception of educators. Misha stood before her students, her heart swelling with a newfound sense of dignity. Recognition began to trickle in as local media covered their initiative—features that celebrated the teachers who inspired change rather than merely existing in the shadows.

In the end, the fight was not merely for pay checks or accolades. It was a journey toward acceptance and recognition, not just for Misha but for all who dared to dream in a space where their efforts often went unnoticed.

As she continued to stand in front of her class, Misha realized that sometimes, the fight for existence meant nurturing hope, not just for oneself, but for an entire generation ready to break free from the confines of indifference. She was a teacher, a trainer, a coach, and in her heart, she was finally becoming what she had always wanted to be—a beacon of dignity in a world that desperately needed it.

Article

Overcoming Helplessness: A Story of Survival

When faced with hardship, the sense of inadequacy can be devastating. It is a normal human reaction to difficult circumstances that appear overwhelming.

Yet, history and personal stories are replete with examples of individuals who have turned their helplessness into a driving force for survival.

This transformation is often marked by resilience, determination, and the will to persevere against all odds.

The Nature of Helplessness

Helplessness arises when a person perceives a lack of control over their circumstances, leading to a state of despair and inaction. There are numerous things that might cause it, such as:
Sudden life changes

- Loss or trauma
- Chronic stress or illness
- Overwhelming responsibilities

The key to overcoming helplessness lies in recognizing these feelings and taking initiative-taking steps to regain a sense of agency.

Strategies for Survival
1.Acceptance and Acknowledgment
The first step in overcoming helplessness is acknowledging its presence. Accepting the situation does not mean giving up; rather, it involves recognizing the challenge and the emotions it evokes, allowing for a clearer path forward.

2. Building Resilience
Resilience is the ability to bounce back from adversity which nurtures through:

- **Mindfulness and Reflection**: Practicing mindfulness helps in staying grounded and focused on the present, reducing anxiety about the future.
- **Positive Relationships**: Surrounding oneself with supportive friends and family provides emotional strength and encouragement.
- **Setting Realistic Goals**: Breaking down overwhelming tasks into manageable steps can restore a sense of control and achievement.

3. Seeking Help and Resources
No one must face their struggles alone. Reaching out for help, whether through therapy, support groups, or community resources, can offer guidance and support. Connecting with those who have faced similar challenges can also provide valuable insights and inspiration.

4. Developing a Survival Mindset
A survival mindset characterized by adaptability, creativity, and a focus on solutions rather than problems. This can be

cultivated by:

Embracing Change: Viewing change as an opportunity for growth rather than a threat.

Problem- Solving Skills: Tackling challenges with a solution-oriented approach.

Self-Compassion: Being kind to oneself during difficult times, recognizing that struggle is a part of the human experience.

Conclusion

Helplessness is a powerful emotion, but it does not have to be a permanent state. By acknowledging its presence and employing strategies to regain control, individuals can transform their sense of helplessness into a catalyst for survival. Through resilience, support, and an initiative-taking mindset, it is possible to navigate even the most challenging of circumstances and emerge stronger than before.